# French Alps and Italian Roads

# French Alps and Italian Roads

Audrey Rey



ISBN: 978-1-304-55823-7

*French Alps and Italian Roads* is also available in e-book format.

For the hours I spent looking at the flowing Italian countryside.

For the Alps that will never cease to astonish me.

And for you, ever present in my thoughts.

**I think about the**

fields of lives
passing instants
blurred by the speed of
the highway
I think about the
fields of lives
and you planted somewhere
in those crossroads
pinpointed by
words
and images you
project to the
anonymous public
including me

**I would kidnap you**

Renault twingo driving
down Italian
roads
rent a house
or
just a room
keep you there
keep us there
stacked bottles of wine
and some fine
cuisine
smoking cigarettes with
an evening view

**There's something about the**

way we both escape
to the mountains
your outlines near a
night's campfire
me on the balcony with
a glass of chardonnay
your hikes
my skiing
your forests
and
my alps
a fragment of an element
drawing us together
connected by the
atoms of
alpine
air

**Mountaintops dipped**

in snow

a guitar playing in

the distance of the summer heat

also

muffled babies' cries

sounds of families'

vacations

keeps me thinking

why not us?

## Pain au chocolat

standing in the isle
choosing the
right bottle of wine
from shelves and shelves
of excellence
wishing you'd be
the one to
open it in the
evening's breeze
amidst Camel
cigarettes
in the sensation
of the intimacy that
could be ours

**I don't know what it**

is

why certain places

act as an amplifier for

empathy

an accelerant for

implanting how much

you miss someone

in one's mind

I don't know whether

it's the slight

reference of being linked

with matter greater

than you

or

maybe it's simply the

immense beauty

of how I am situated

at this

bottom valley

point

looking at the

rising alps

in 360° view

that makes me miss

every single aspect

shape
angle
of you

## Not the ocean

it's over 2000m
that I feel
release
melancholy release
from being pinpointed
in every view of
my vivacious
day-to-day life
in such atmosphere
in the thinning air
I separate trivialities
with ease
but have an even
more deafening yearning
for what could be pillars
for what could be reasons
for me to keep
going on

**Well, shit,**

do you even realize …

… no …

*could* you even imagine

how fulfilling this

apartment would be

with our bodies

transitioning through

rooms

through meals

and

time?

Could you even imagine

just how easy it would

be

if you let go of all

inner controls

and detour the

check-points

coming to me?

**Laughing about**

my stalker intentions
because you know
you've got them too.
These few moments
of unsupervised sincerity
of below-the-radar
truthfulness
surpass the veil
of you trying to
keep me away.

**Italian bikers**

Russian skiers
and French rugby players
on the field
the passing glances
the *bonjour* smiles
and an audience
when I ski
hot afternoons turn into
windy evenings
one last walk around
the lake
hidden below the covers
straight from under the
shower
you in
an indirect message
directed directly
towards me

**I'm having fun,**

I really am,
I hope our childish games
have the same
effect on you.
I hope you smile
when you think
my words were
meant for you.

**You're naming things**

making lists
shouting out
what you desire
making plans
staring into
the stone mountains
I let the snow melt
through my fingers
and I feel all you want
and I see
that most of
my life's pretty little
boxes
have been checked
so why do you act
like I couldn't offer
couldn't give
what you
need

## You're in my head

your smile
your hands
even the way you
smoke
the snores that let
me know you're fast
asleep
and the gratitude in your
eyes when I
serve you breakfast
you're in my skin
your kisses
and caresses
and the way you
hug me
hold me
longer
feeling me with all
that you are
so you see
honey
you're with me
forever

no distance can

be

too far.

**You have an artistic**

mind
I do too.
I guess that's one of
the reasons we
get along
like we do.
But artistic minds
are capable of
creating endless
worlds
and
conflicts
and
fictitious truths
and our joint projects
can easily become
each other's
b-sides.

## Yes

it gets confusing
making contact
in a dead zone
in *our* dead zone
yes
it's not linear
logical
predictable
but I'd choose
these unmarked mountain
paths
over geometrical
concrete
every
every
time

**Not knowing how to act**

around you,
you could say it's part
of the charm,
and after the currents
of words pass
my mind is nude,
full but silent.
And I feel free
within the confines of you.

**Sometimes it's like**

we're standing in
a room of mirrors
our distorted
images interacting
in numerous reflections
of fragments of
our thoughts
our fears
and blurring the
desires
we could have
fulfilled

**When it comes to you**

I can't help myself

I've never been this

attached

to someone's flaws

**Roy Orbison**

is dictating my days
but at least I cry
less
I think
yes
Roy
can narrate my nights
can sing my
living for you

**Waterfalls**

lakes
villages hidden
in the pores of mountains
and it feels like
you're with me
with every step
dissolving
frustrations
with every artistic
photo you take

**I despise these**

frightened feelings
I get when I check
my calendar
how many days till
I head home
I feel that this distance
brought us closer
almost more than
we were before
I'll miss waking up
amidst sun-dipped mountains
smiling because they
remind me of you
and I fear the night
I'll fall asleep
without almost lucidly
feeling
you

**I wish I could take**

you
across country lines
and up the spiral
roads
I wish you'd know
that I wouldn't mind
leaving urban
excitement and
metropolitan lights
behind for you

**Maybe I know of a**

way we could

make it …

But are you willing

to run away?

**You've sent me songs**

so many songs
I can relate too
through you
for you
because of you

**As much as I laugh**

at my friends' requests
to blow off some
steam or
to have reckless fun
I have to disagree when
it comes to
holding a grudge
I wish you'd experience
the serenity that slipped
through the
windows with
every turn around
the mountain
or walk around
the windy surface
of the lake
I wish you'd feel how
easy the afternoon is
in the bordeaux's
aroma
filling the kitchen
and releasing itself
through all the rooms
I wish you'd feel this
unconditional love for

someone
that I feel for you

**I would love nothing**
more but to tell
you
how I am
in love
with your receding
hairline
but it would only
make you feel old
I desire so badly to
show you how much
everything about you
yes
your age too
turns me on

**Cold jeans and**

hot blue skies
and Mont Blanc proudly
risen
over tourist driven
streets
strong espresso
time stops in the shade
your silhouette occupies the
vacant seat
smiling and lighting
cigarettes
the small cup in your
hands
your feet bumping
against mine

**Progressively more**

detached from reality
I let myself flow through
the pine trees
evaporate in you

**It would be**

unimaginably beautiful
to be able to share
these views
and feelings with
you
to fall asleep in
your arms
with the cold
evening air
stealing urban difficulties

**I was never close with**

impressionists
but the highest
parts of nature
are what pure beauty
is
I feel inspiration
filling my lungs
letting me breathe
truly breathe
in the way
I feel you running
through my veins
I am living on
the essence
of art

**Your initials tattooed**

on my fingers
your name
where my wedding
ring should be
maybe will be
once
someday

**And then I'm passing**

all these Italian

villages

again

imagining a glass of

chianti

with you

**Let the image**

of us

in a vineyard

overflow your mind

blinded by the

Veneto sun

**I'd pull off the**

highway

take you to one

of these

motels

with orange

facades

white windows

isolated rooms

**I will love**

you

eternally

like serenity

rests

upon the

glaciers

www.ingramcontent.com/pod-product-compliance
Ingram Content Group UK Ltd.
Pitfield, Milton Keynes, MK11 3LW, UK
UKHW020229250726
13967UKWH00001B/263